Dao De Jing

The Way

and

Virtuous Power

Dao De Jing- The Way and Virtuous Power

ISBN 978-1532906084

Version 1.2

Connect on Facebook
www.facebook.com/TheWayAndVirtuousPower
or find more info on
www.dao-de-jing.dk

道 Dao

The Universe is ever expanding

Expansion creates motion

like an unending flowing river

德 De

I cannot make a tree blossom when I want it to

I cannot make it bear fruit before it is time

I can choose where to plant the seed

I can nurture it and protect it

I can watch it the few days it blossoms

I can enjoy the fruit when it is ripe

Then I must wait until next year

Lars Bo - 2016

Preface

We know today that the Dao De Jing is at least 2300 years old. The oldest excavated copy was found in 1993 in Guodian in the Hubei province. It was written on bamboo strips and has been dated to around 300 BCE. Written sources state the Dao De Jing to be from the 6th century BCE, which may very well be true.
However, the author cannot be verified with certainty. We assume it was a man and that he was later known as The Old Master - Lao Zi. Some accounts of his life and real name are clearly only mythical, but others seem much more realistic. A great deal of thorough research has been done on this matter but this is not the place to repeat it. The Dao De Jing has survived and achieved praise and respect for more than two millennium - and it will continue to be so. In that way you could say its success has made the search for its author redundant.

Dao De Jing is a very inspiring book and many millions have read it. Some say it is political other say it is spiritual - Personally I would say that it is both. My own view is that The Way is as a force of life in the universe that is not personified. But there may be an infinite number of other interpretations of what the Way is. In fact, I do not think we should try to make a standard interpretation for The Way. If a loyal and precise translation is provided I believe most people will find some truth in this book, and truth can always be perceived on different levels and from different angles just like the bird talking about the wonders of the four seasons and the grasshopper angrily claiming there are only three - because no grasshopper has ever seen winter.

I have often read people mention the humour in the Dao De Jing and often wise and original words and ideas will make you smile. However, I don't believe the author intended to be funny in any part of the text. The book is full of sincere opinions on how to govern a state, ideas about war and killing, corruption, arrogance, survival of the fittest, good reasons to be a coward in war. Furthermore, besides The Way itself there are serene observations and advice about cosmology, yin-yang, the power of the female energy, softness, humbleness, pacifism, and beautiful thoughts on peace as a prerequisite for prosperity and much more. But foremost, the Dao De Jing is known for the idea of 'non-action'. This is not the same as letting everything go wrong, but letting everything find its natural course. This is brilliantly illustrated with the famous analogy: *'Ruling a large country is like cooking a small fish'* - if you stir too much the delicate fish gets ruined.

It is an undisputable fact that different people praise different translations that give diverse or even completely opposite ideas and conclusions. The differences in the existing translations are often quite dramatic and this means that it is far from possible to say that there exists an authoritative translation. However, among the scholarly translations the differences are, in fact, not so dramatic. After reading one of the better translations the reader will in broad terms be able to understand the message of the Dao De Jing. There are a few important points in the original that I hope to be able to clear up, and I sincerely hope I can assist the reader in coming to a deeper and more precise understanding of this wise and wonderful book.

A great deal has been written about the excavated Mawangdui and Guodian versions. But the excavated versions have in general not given much reason for different interpretations and in general we seem to have a quite reliable original to work with.
Some have argued that they believe the Dao De Jing to be a collection of texts from many different authors - this is not my view. The ideas described may seem strange and incoherent to some people but I find them inspiring, brilliant and very coherent.
This translation is based on the Wang Bi version. A small number of notes are found at the end of the book.
The text is written in the times of an ancient culture and it is, in my opinion, not possible to make a gender neutral translation.
The dictionary used is *Hanyu Da Cidian.*
Finally I will express my gratitude to Stella Sørensen for correcting my English.

Dao

道可道
非常道
名可名
非常名
無名天地之始
有名萬物之母
故常無欲
以觀其妙
常有欲
以觀其徼
此兩者
同出而異名
同謂之玄
玄之又玄
眾妙之門

道

The Way can lead somewhere
but it is not a common road
A name can name it
but it is not a common name[1]
It has no name and is the beginning of Heaven and Earth
It is called the mother of the myriads of things
Thus it is that those who are always without desires
will see its excellence
Those who always have desires will merely see its outline
These two arise from the same source
but have different names
Their common origin is profound
Infinitely profound indeed
It is the gate of the myriads of wonders

天下皆知美之為美
斯惡已
皆知善之為善
斯不善已
故有無相生
難易相成
長短相較
高下相傾
音聲相和
前後相隨
是以聖人處無為之事
行不言之教
萬物作焉而不辭
生而不有
為而不恃
功成而弗居
夫唯弗居
是以不去

道

Everyone in the world knows that beauty is beautiful
but this means ugliness must already exist
Everyone knows goodness is good
but this means not good must already exist
So it is that being and not being create each other
Difficult and easy complete each other
Long and short contrast each other
High and low stretch toward each other
Music and song harmonize each other
Front and back follow each other
Therefore the wise person manages affairs without taking action
and engages in teaching without words
Creates everything without saying a word about it
Gives life but is not possessive
Acts without expectations
Completes the task but does not linger
Precisely because by not lingering it will not go away

不尚賢使民不爭
不貴難得之貨使民不為盜
不見可欲使心不亂
是以聖人之治虛其心
實其腹
弱其志
強其骨
常使民無知無欲
使夫知者不敢為也
為無為則無不治

道

By not praising abilities people will not contend
By not making rare things valuable people will not steal
By not displaying the desirable
the heart will not be confused
Thus the wise person's Way of ruling people is
to to empty their hearts
to fill their stomachs
to weaken their ambitions
to strengthen their bones
to always keep people unaware and without desires
to make people who are aware of these things afraid to act
He acts without actions thereby governing all

道沖而用之或不盈
淵兮
似萬物之宗
挫其銳
解其紛
和其光
同其塵
湛兮似或存
吾不知誰之子
象帝之先

道

4

The Way is empty
yet it can be used without being refilled
It is an infinite abyss
that could be the ancestor of all things
It softens the edges
Untangles the entangled
Softens the sunlight
Settles the dust
It is deep like our very existence
I do not know who it is the child of
It appears to precede God

天地不仁
以萬物為芻狗
聖人不仁
以百姓為芻狗
天地之間
其猶橐籥乎
虛而不屈
動而愈出
多言數窮
不如守中

道

5

Heaven and Earth are not kindhearted
they treat all things as straw dogs[2]
The wise person is not kindhearted
but treats people like straw dogs
The space between Heaven and Earth
is it not like bellows and pipe?
Empty when not pressed together
when moved more and more comes out
Many words are often spent
but that is not as good as keeping the centre

谷神不死
是謂玄牝
玄牝之門
是謂天地根
綿綿若存
用之不勤

道

6

The spirit of the valley never dies
it is called the dark female
The dark female is a gate
it is called the root of Heaven and Earth
It is ever so soft
use it gently

天長地久
天地所以能長且久者
以其不自生
故能長生
是以聖人後其身而身先
外其身而身存
非以其無私耶
故能成其私

Heaven is eternal and Earth everlasting
The reason they can be eternal and everlasting is
that they do not give life to themselves
Thus they can have long life
Therefore the wise person stays behind but is in front
Stays outside but is there
Is it not because he is selfless
that he can complete what he wants?

上善若水
水善利萬物而不爭
處眾人之所惡
故幾於道
居善地
心善淵
與善仁
言善信
正善治
事善能
動善時
夫唯不爭
故無尤

道

7

Water has the highest excellence
Its excellence is that it benefits everything without resistance[3]
It can be in places that all people disdain
therefore it is near to The Way
For a house excellence is standing on the ground
For the heart excellence is to be like a deep pond
In being together excellence is benevolence
When talking excellence is being trustworthy
In governing excellence is order
In managing affairs excellence is ability
In moving excellence is timing
But only because there is no resistance there are no faults

持而盈之
不如其已
揣而銳之
不可長保
金玉滿堂
莫之能守
富貴而驕
自遺其咎
功遂身退天之道

To hold it steady and fill it to the brim
is not as good as stopping a little short
Shaping it with a hammer and sharpening it
will not make it defend you forever
If the chambers are filled with gold and jade
no one can protect it
If riches and honour make you arrogant
it will carry the punishment in itself
Simply retiring after the job is done well
that is The Way of Heaven

載營魄抱一，能無離乎？專氣致柔，能嬰兒乎？滌除玄覽，能無疵乎？愛民治國，能無知乎？天門開闔，能為雌乎？明白四達，能無知乎？生之畜之，生而不有，為而不恃，長而不宰，是謂玄德。

道

Fully integrate your soul and keep it as one
Can you avoid that it splits up?
When you focus your energy and make it soft
can you be like a baby?
If you clean the dirty mirror
can you make it spotless?
When you care for the people and rule the country
can you do it without being clever?
When the Gate of Heaven opens and closes
can you act with the feminine aspect?
When you understand everything
can you abstain from using insight?
Give life and nurture it
but give life without possessing it
Act without expectations
Be senior without demanding leadership
This is what we call the elusive Virtuous Power

三十輻
共一轂
當其無
有車之用
埏埴以為器
當其無
有器之用
鑿戶牖
以為室
當其無
有室之用
故有之以為利
無之以為用

道

Thirty spokes
connected in a hub
Distributing the spaces between them
is what makes the carriage of good use
Clay is kneaded into a pot
Balancing the space inside
is what makes the pot usable
We cut holes for doors and windows
and consider it a house
The right spaces
are what makes the house habitable
Therefore what is there is of value
But what is not there can also be useful

五色令人目盲
五音令人耳聾
五味令人口爽
馳騁田獵
令人心發狂
難得之貨
令人行妨
是以聖人為腹不為目
故去彼取此

道

The five colours blind people's eyes
The five tones deafen people's ears
The five tastes dulls people's taste
To gallop on a hunt can make people overexcited
Rare things hinder people's progress
Thus the wise person cares for the stomach
but not the eye
Therefore some things are rejected
and others are accepted

寵辱若驚
貴大患若身
何謂寵辱若驚
寵為下
得之若驚失之若驚
是謂寵辱若驚
何謂貴大患若身
吾所以有大患者為吾有身
及吾無身吾有何患
故貴以身為天下
若可寄天下
愛以身為天下
若可託天下

道

Honour and disgrace are both upsetting
Value great misfortune as much as you value yourself
What is meant by 'honour and disgrace are both upsetting'?
Honour is given to people below
It upsets them when they get it and also if they lose it
This is what is meant by
'honour and disgrace are both upsetting'
What is meant by
'value great misfortune as much as you value yourself'?
What causes me to have great misfortune is that I have a self
If I had no self what misfortune could I have?
Therefore placing value in seeing yourself as the whole world
means you can be entrusted the world
Affectionately seeing yourself as the whole world
means the world can be trusted in your care

視之不見名曰夷
聽之不聞名曰希
搏之不得名曰微
此三者不可致詰
故混而為一
其上不皦
其下不昧
繩繩不可名
復歸於無物
是謂無狀之狀
無物之象
是謂惚恍
迎之不見其首
隨之不見其後
執古之道
以御今之有
能知古始
是謂道紀

Looking without seeing is called being unenlightened
Listening without hearing is called prejudice
What you try to grab but cannot reach is called subtle
These three cannot be defined further
However they are one and the same
Above it is not bright
Below it is not dark
It can never be named
It goes back to nothingness
This is called
the formless form
an abstract image
It is shrouded and misty
When you greet it you do not see its face
If you follow it you do not see its back
By adhering to the Way of the ancients
you can control what is today
If you can understand the ancient beginning
that is the chronicle of the Way

古之善為士者微妙玄通
深不可識
夫唯不可識
故強為之容
豫兮若冬涉川
猶兮若畏四鄰
儼兮其若客
渙兮若冰之將釋
敦兮其若樸
曠兮其若谷
混兮其若濁
孰能濁以靜之徐清
孰能安以久動之徐生
保此道者不欲盈
夫唯不盈故能蔽不新成

道

The brilliance of the ancient scholars
were subtle and profound
So deep it is hard to realize
We can only try our best to comprehend
They were
Farsighted like crossing a river in winter
Careful like in enemy territory
Polite like being a guest
Unassuming like melting ice
Sincere like uncarved wood
Wide like a valley
Complicated like a muddled pool
Who can be muddled and slowly clear it with silence?
Who can be peaceful and move it slowly out into life?
Those who maintain this Way
do not desire much of anything
This is why they can look ragged
and do not strive for new achievements

致虛極守靜篤
萬物並作吾以觀復
夫物芸芸各復歸其根
歸根曰靜是謂復命
復命曰常知常曰明
不知常妄作凶
知常容容乃公
公乃王王乃天
天乃道道乃久
沒身不殆

Extend emptiness to the utmost
carefully guard your silence
All things rise together
and I see them return
They bloom in abundance
then each return to their root
To return to the root is stillness
this is to revive life
That life can be revived means it is everlasting
Knowing this is called enlightenment
Not knowing that life is everlasting
you have no direction of your actions and this is not good
Knowing that life is everlasting makes you magnanimous
One who is magnanimous
can come to have the bearing of a duke
One who has the bearing of a duke
can come to have the bearing of a king
Having the bearing of a king leads to Heaven
Heaven leads to The Way
The Way leads to eternity
The end of your body is not dangerous

太上下知有之
其次親而譽之
其次畏之
其次侮之
信不足焉有不信焉
悠兮其貴言
功成事遂
百姓皆謂我自然

道

The highest ruler is known to those below
The next in rank they love and praise
The next after this in rank they fear
The next rank down they mock
Without being trustworthy there is mistrust
Carefully place value in your words
and complete all affairs satisfactorily
Then people will all say you handle things with ease

廢義出偽不慈昏亂
道仁慧大親孝家忠
大有智有六有國有
臣昏慈不偽出義廢

大道廢有仁義
智慧出有大偽
六親不和有孝慈
國家昏亂有忠臣

道

When the Great Way was abandoned
benevolence and righteousness arose
Wisdom and intelligence came forward
because there was great misconception
When families were not in harmony
filial piety and loving parents came into being
Chaos in the country
caused there to be loyal subjects

絕聖棄智
民利百倍
絕仁棄義
民復孝慈
絕巧棄利
盜賊無有
此三者以為文不足
故令有所屬
見素抱樸
少私寡欲
絕學無憂

道

Stop using wisdom and discard knowledge
it will benefit the people hundredfold
Stop being benevolent and abstain from righteousness
then people will go back to filial piety and parental love
Reject tricks and abstain from benefit
then robbers and bandits will not exist
It is not sufficient to write these three points
They must be combined with
Seeing the simple and embracing the plain
Moderate selfishness and reduce desires
Stop learning and have no worries[4]

唯之與阿相去幾何
善之與惡相去若何
人之所畏不可不畏
荒兮其未央哉
眾人熙熙
如享太牢如春登臺
我獨怕兮其未兆
如嬰兒之未孩
儽儽兮若無所歸
眾人皆有餘而我獨若遺
我愚人之心也哉沌沌兮
俗人昭昭我獨若昏
俗人察察我獨悶悶
澹兮其若海飂兮若無止
眾人皆有以而我獨頑似鄙
我獨異於人而貴食母

道

20

How big is the difference between 'yeah' and 'aye'? [5]
How far apart is good and bad?
What other people fear I must also fear
The desolation is endless!
Everyone is ever so happy
just like when they perform the Great Sacrifice
or ascend the alter in the spring
Only I feel lost without any good omens
Like a baby who will not live to become a child
So fatigued! like being homeless
Everyone has more than they need
only I have lost everything
My foolish heart! I am so confused
Ordinary people are clearheaded
only I am clouded
Ordinary people see clearly
only I am muddled
Drifting like the ocean
blowing around like there is nowhere to settle
Everyone has a purpose
only I seem misplaced
Only I am different
I wish I was back at my mother's breast

45

孔德之容唯道是從
道之為物唯恍唯惚
忽兮恍兮其中有象
恍兮忽兮其中有物
窈兮冥兮其中有精
其精甚真其中有信
自古及今其名不去
以閱眾甫
吾何以知眾甫之狀哉
以此

道

The grandest power can only come from the Way
The description of The Way is obscure and elusive
Elusive and obscure
but there is a shape in it
Obscure and elusive
but there is substance in it
Deep and profound
but there is an essence in it
This essence is very real
there is truth in it
From ancient times up until now its name was not lost
Through it you can see all origins
How can I know the shape of all origins?
With this!

曲則全枉則直
窪則盈弊則新
少則得多則惑
是以聖人抱一
為天下式
不自見故明
不自是故彰
不自伐故有功
不自矜故長
夫唯不爭
故天下莫能與之爭
古之所謂曲則全者
豈虛言哉
誠全而歸之

22

If it is round it is complete
If it is crooked it will be straightened out
If it is hollow it will be filled
If it is falling apart it will be replaced
If it has too little it will gain
If there are many it will be confusing
Therefore the wise person holds oneness
as the guiding principle for everything in the world
Not showing off thereby giving a clear impression
Not claiming to be correct and is therefore recognized
Not bragging and therefore holds a reputation
Is not overly confident and therefore lives longer
Precisely because he does not dispute
in all the world no one is able to argue with him
What the ancients said about 'round is complete'
were certainly not empty words!

希言自然
故飄風不終朝
驟雨不終日
孰為此者天地
天地尚不能久
而況於人乎
故從事於道者
道者同於道
德者同於德
失者同於失
同於道者道亦樂得之
同於德者德亦樂得之
同於失者失亦樂得之
信不足焉有不信焉

道

23

Being of few words is a natural thing
Just like a whirlwind does not last all morning
A shower does not last all day
Why is it so? It is Heaven and Earth
If Heaven and Earth cannot be long lasting
how can human beings?
So for those who conduct their affairs following The Way
it is like this
Those who follow The Way are aligned with The Way
Those who are powerful are aligned with Power
Those who lose The Way are aligned with being lost
When you are aligned with The Way it welcomes you
When you are aligned with Power it welcomes you
When you are aligned with being lost
loss is readily experienced
Those who do not trust enough will not be trusted

企者不立
跨者不行
自見者不明
自是者不彰
自伐者無功
自矜者不長
其在道也曰
餘食贅行
物或惡之
故有道者不處

道

24

Those who stand on toes are not upright
Those who stride do not walk
Those who show themselves
do not give a clear impression
Those who claim to be correct are not recognized
Those who brag do not hold a reputation
Those who are over confident will not live long
From the standpoint of The Way this could be said to be
like excessive nourishment and needless actions
Everyone dislikes that
Therefore those who possess The Way
would not be in this position

有物混成
先天地生
寂兮寥兮
獨立不改
周行而不殆
可以為天下母
吾不知其名字之曰道
強為之名曰大
大曰逝
逝曰遠
遠曰反
故道大天大地大王亦大
域中有四大而王居其一焉
人法地
地法天
天法道
道法自然

道

25

There was something that came together and formed
It was born before Heaven and Earth
How silent and lonely
Independent and unchanging
It moved all over but was never in danger
We can say it was the mother of all under Heaven
I do not know its name but to name it I call it The Way
If I had to give it a name it would be Great
We say that greatness passes away
We say that what passes away is far
We say that what is far will return
Therefore The Way is great
Heaven is great
The Earth is great
The King is great
In the land there are four great ones
and the king is one of them
Humans are shaped by the Earth
The Earth is shaped by Heaven
Heaven is shaped by The Way
The Way was shaped by itself

重為輕根
靜為躁君
是以聖人終日行不離輜重
雖有榮觀燕處超然
奈何萬乘之主而以身輕天下
輕則失本躁則失君

Heavy is the root of light
Calm is the ruler of restless
Therefore the wise person is traveling all day
without leaving the wagon
Even if there are great things to see
he remains idle and detached
How can the leader of a great fleet of chariots
regard himself to be of light importance in the world?
Being light you have lost your root
Being restless you have lost the command

善行無轍迹
善言無瑕讁
善數不用籌策
善閉無關楗而不可開
善結無繩約而不可解
是以聖人常善救人
故無棄人
常善救物
故無棄物
是謂襲明
故善人者
不善人之師
不善人者
善人之資
不貴其師
不愛其資
雖智大迷
是謂要妙

The skilful traveler does not leave tracks
The eloquent speaker says nothing he can be reproached for
The skilful reckoner needs no tally stick
One who is smart when closing a door has no need to bolt it
yet the door cannot be opened
One who is good at tying does not need to make a knot
yet it cannot be untied
This is how the wise person
is always good at saving people
and thus no one is abandoned
Always good at saving things
and thus nothing is discarded
This is making practical use of insight
Thus the skilful is the teacher for the unskilled
The unskilled is the raw material for the skilful
If you do not value your teacher
the teacher is not fond of his material
so even if you are intelligent you will be greatly confused
This is the important thing about being clever

知其雄守其雌
為天下谿
為天下谿
常德不離
復歸於嬰兒
知其白守其黑
為天下式
為天下式
常德不忒
復歸於無極
知其榮守其辱
為天下谷
為天下谷
常德乃足
復歸於樸
樸散則為器
聖人用之則為官長
故大制不割

道

Know the male qualities but keep the female qualities
then you will be a river valley in the world
If you are like a river valley
the constant Virtuous Power will never leave
and you will be like a new born again
Know white but keep black
and you will be a role model for the world
If you are a role model for the world
the always present Virtuous Power will not fail
and you will return to nothingness
Know glory but keep humble
then you will be a valley in the world
If you are a valley in the world
the Virtuous Power will be ample
and you will return to your unprocessed state of being
When raw material is broken loose it becomes useful
The wise person uses this when employed as superior
for the officials
The great way of managing is to not cut into shape

將欲取天下而為之
吾見其不得已
天下神器不可為也
為者敗之執者失之
故物
或行或隨
或歔或吹
或強或羸
或挫或隳
是以聖人
去甚去奢去泰

道

30

Those who assist the ruler of the people by using The Way
do not use weapons to force the world
Such affairs can easily rebound
Where an army camps thistles and thorns grow
When a big army leaves
there will inevitably be a year of famine
The clever stops as soon as there is a result
He does not dare to stay and consolidate the position
He gets the result but is not overly confident
He gets the result but does not slaughter the enemy
He gets the result but is not arrogant
He gets the result only because he does not have a choice
He gets the result without consolidating his forces
When things have grown strong
they are already becoming old
This is not following The Way
He who does not follow The Way will perish soon

夫佳兵者不祥之器
物或惡之故有道者不處
君子居則貴左用兵則貴右
兵者不祥之器非君子之器
不得已而用之恬淡為上
勝而不美而美之者
是樂殺人夫樂殺人者
則不可以得志於天下矣
吉事尚左凶事尚右
偏將軍居左上將軍居右
言以喪禮處之
殺人之眾以哀悲泣之
戰勝以喪禮處之

道

31

Fine weapons are ominous tools
Most beings dislike them and therefore those
who possess The Way will not rely on this
When the nobleman is at home he values the left side
When he is resorting to arms he values the right side
Fine weapons are ominous tools not suitable for a nobleman
He wields them only when there is no other option
But then keeps a neutral attitude
When he wins he is not happy about it
If he was it would be happiness over killing people
He who is happy about killing people
cannot attain his worldly ambitions
Good affairs are praised as the left side
Bad affairs is praised as the right side
The second in command is on the left side
The commander in chief is on the right side
It can thus be said
that the right side is the place of the funeral rite
Having killed many people
makes you weep with grief and compassion for them
He who wins a battle regards it as a funeral ritual

道常無名
樸雖小天下莫能臣也
侯王若能守之萬物將自賓
天地相合以降甘露
民莫之令而自均
始制有名
名亦既有夫亦將知止
知止所以不殆
譬道之在天下
猶川谷之與江海

道

32

The Way was forever nameless
Crude and small
but no one in the world can make it their subject
If lords and kings could hold it
all beings would come to stay of their own will
Heaven and Earth would unite and send down sweet dew
and without being ordered people would feel equal
When beginning to exert control there will be names
Already when there are names
you should realize it is time to stop
Knowing it is time to stop will call off the danger
The Way in the world can be illustrated by how
a valley stream can have a hand
in creating the river and the ocean

知人者智
自知者明
勝人者有力
自勝者強
知足者富
強行者有志
不失其所者久
死而不亡者壽

道

33

To know other people is knowledge
To know yourself is enlightenment
To defeat other people is power
To defeat yourself is strength
To know how to be content is wealth
Powerful action is will
Not losing your position is to stay long
To die but not perish is eternal life[7]

大道汎兮其可左右
萬物恃之而生而不辭
功成不名有
衣養萬物而不為主
常無欲可名於小
萬物歸焉而不為主
可名為大
以其終不自為大
故能成其大

道

The Great Way is floating everywhere like a mist
All living creatures depend on it
to give them life without conditions
The results are achieved but it makes no claim
It clothes and feeds all living creatures
but does claim to be their ruler
It never desires anything
and can be counted among the small
All creatures rely on it
but does not regard it as their ruler
It can be said to be great
But because it never regards itself as great
it can fulfil its greatness

執大象天下往
往而不害
安平大
樂與餌過客止
道之出口淡乎其無味
視之不足見聽之不足聞
用之不足既

道

35

Holding The Great Image the world will follow
They follow along and do not come to harm
and there will be great peace
Music and good food makes the passersby stop
But when someone speaks The Way
everything else seem tasteless
Watching is not sufficient to see it
Listening is not sufficient to hear it
To use it is not sufficient to use it up

將欲歙之必固張之
將欲弱之必固強之
將欲廢之必固興之
將欲奪之必固與之
是謂微明
柔弱勝剛強
魚不可脫於淵
國之利器不可以示人

道

36

If you want to draw it in you must extend it out
If you want to weaken it you must strengthen it
If you want it to fall you must raise it
If you want to take you must give
This is understanding the subtle
The soft and powerless conquer the hard and strong
Fish cannot escape the pond
The country's fine weapons should not be shown to people

道常無為而無不為
侯王若能守之
萬物將自化
化而欲作
吾將鎮之以無名之樸
無名之樸夫亦將無欲
不欲以靜
天下將自定

道

37

The Way never acts but leaves nothing undone
If the lords and the king can hold it
all things will develop by itself
While things develop the urge to interfere might crop up
but then I suppress it with the nameless resource
The nameless resource assists you in having no desires
Having no desires gives you serenity
and everything will fall into place by itself

De

德

上德不德是以有德
下德不失德是以無德
上德無為而無以為
下德為之而有以為
上仁為之而無以為
上義為之而有以為
上禮為之而莫之應
則攘臂而扔之
故失道而後德
失德而後仁
失仁而後義
失義而後禮
夫禮者忠信之薄而亂之首
前識者道之華而愚之始
是以大丈夫處其厚不居其薄
處其實不居其華
故去彼取此

德

38

The highest form of power is to not apply power
this makes it Virtuous Power[8]
The lower form of power clings to power
and is therefore not Virtuous Power
The highest form of power is to take no action
but leaving nothing undone
The lower form of power is to wield it
when there is a reason
The highest form of benevolence is to act with it
when there is a reason
The highest form of righteousness is to apply it
when there is a reason
The highest rituals are performed
but no one responds to them
That is what happens when we "pull up our sleeves and act!"
And thus throw it all away
This is how
The Way is lost and power follows in its wake
Virtuous Power is lost and righteousness follow in its wake
righteousness is lost and rituals follows in its wake
Rituals are a facade of honesty and loyalty
and the prelude to disorder
Knowing things in advance is one of the gains of The Way
but also how fools start out
Therefore a man of integrity stays with what has substance
and avoids the superficial
He relies on facts not on intuition
He gets rid of some things but keeps others

昔之得一者
天得一以清
地得一以寧
神得一以靈
谷得一以盈
萬物得一以生
侯王得一以為天下貞
其致之
天無以清將恐裂
地無以寧將恐發
神無以靈將恐歇
谷無以盈將恐竭
萬物無以生將恐滅
侯王無以貴高將恐蹶
故貴以賤為本高以下為基
是以侯王自稱孤寡不穀
此非以賤為本耶非乎
故致數譽無譽
不欲琭琭如玉珞珞如石

德

39

In past times these attained oneness
Heaven attained oneness and had clarity
Earth attained oneness and had peace
Spirit attained oneness and had intelligence
The valley attained oneness and was filled
All creatures under Heaven attained their oneness and was born
The lords and kings attained oneness a
nd could keep everything in order
The cause of this is that
A Heaven that is not clear may crack
The Earth without peace may erupt
Spirit without intelligence may vanish
The valley without something to fill it may empty
If everything is not born the world may die out
If lords and kings do not value high rank they may lose it
Therefore lords regard humbleness as the root
High regards low as foundation
This is why lords and kings use overly humble names
to refer to themselves
Does this not mean they regard humbleness as their foundation?
Certainly!
To them the finest praise is no praise
They do not desire to be adored like jade
or to be as unassailable as stone

反者道之動
弱者道之用
天下萬物生於有
有生於無

德

Ever returning is the movement of The Way
Softness is how The Way works
All things under Heaven were born into existence
What exists was born in the void

上士聞道
勤而行之
中士聞道
若存若亡
下士聞道
大笑之
不笑不足以為道
故建言有之
明道若昧
進道若退
夷道若纇
上德若谷
太白若辱
廣德若不足
建德若偷
質真若渝
大方無隅
大器晚成
大音希聲
大象無形
道隱無名
夫唯道
善始且成

When superior scholars hear of The Way
they do their best to walk it
When average scholars hear of The Way
they hold it for a while but lose it
When inferior scholars hear of The Way
they laugh loudly
If they were not laughing it would not be The Way
That is why the saying goes
The obvious way seems obscure
The way forward seems to be leading backwards
The even way seems rugged
The highest virtue seems to be in low places[9]
The purest white seems sullied
All embracing virtue is not sufficient
Strong virtue is unreliable
The plain truth seems able to change
A big square does not have corners
A big pot takes time to make
A loud tone may sound faint
A large image has no shape
The Way cannot be seen and has no name
But only The Way is so great that
it can both begin and end things[10]

道生一
一生二
二生三
三生萬
萬物負陰而抱陽
沖氣以為和
人之所惡唯孤寡不穀
而王公以為稱
故物
或損之而益
或益之而損
人之所教我亦教之
強梁者不得其死
吾將以為教父

德

42

One is born of The Way
Two is born of one
Three is born of two
The myriads of worldly things are born from three
The myriads of things carry yin at their back
and hold yang at their chest
They are opposite energies that are in harmony
What people dislike is to be lonely insignificant and miserable
That is why kings and lords refer to themselves by these names
And so it is that some things increase by being decreased
and other things decrease by being increased
What people are teaching me
is exactly what I teach them
Those who use unyielding strength[11]
will not die a natural death
I will consider this the father of my teachings

天下之至柔馳騁天下之至堅
無有入無間
吾是以知無為之有益
不言之教
無為之益
天下希及之

德

43

The softest in the world easily outruns the strongest
What has no substance can enter where there is no room
From this I know that not taking action can be beneficial
Teaching without words and benefit from taking no action
Only few in the world reach this

名與身孰親
身與貨孰多
得與亡孰病
是故甚愛必大費
多藏必厚亡
知足不辱
知止不殆
可以長久

德

Is your name or your body most dear to you?
Is it your body or material things that you value most?
Gain or loss which of them is the problem?
It is so that those who desire intensely always spend a lot
Those who gather much are bound to lose much
Those who know moderation will not meet disgrace
Those who know to stop in time
will not put themselves in danger
and they can live long

大成若缺
其用不弊
大盈若沖
其用不窮
大直若屈
大巧若拙
大辯若訥
躁勝寒靜勝熱
清靜為天下正

德

45

Truly great achievements appear to be incomplete
so they will not be used for bad purposes
Great fullness appear to not pour out
thus it will not be emptied
Great straightness seems bent
Great cleverness seems a little slow
Great eloquence seems inarticulate
Movement defeats cold
Stillness defeats heat
Purity and serenity straightens out everything

天下有道卻走馬以糞
天下無道戎馬生於郊
禍莫大於不知足
咎莫大於欲得
故知足之足常足矣

德

46

If The Way is in the world
horses used for riding will stay home
and be used for spreading manure[12]
If The Way is not in the world
war horses are bread outside the city
The greatest misfortune comes from
not understanding how to be content
The greatest fault is wanting to gain
Therefore the satisfaction that comes from
understanding how to be content
is a lasting satisfaction

不出戶知天下
不闚牖見天道
其出彌遠
其知彌少
是以聖人
不行而知
不見而名
不為而成

德

47

You can know the world without going out the door
You can see Heaven's Way without looking out the window
The farther you go out the less you come to know
This is why the wise person
Does not walk about yet knows what is going on
Does not see yet can describe things
Does not act yet completes matters

為學日益
為道日損
損之又損
以至於無為
無為而無不為
取天下常以無事
及其有事
不足以取天下

Those who study increases day by day
Those who follow The Way decreases day by day
They decrease and further decrease
in order to reach non action
They do not act but leave nothing undone
Those who want to conquer the world
are never engaged in affairs
If they were engaged in affairs
they would not be suited to conquer the world

聖人無常心，
以百姓心為心
善者吾善之
不善者吾亦善之
德善
信者吾信之
不信者吾亦信之
德信
聖人在天下歙歙
為天下渾其心
百姓皆注其耳目
聖人皆孩之

德

49

The wise person has an amenable frame of mind
taking the people's frame of mind as his
Those who are good I see as good
Those who are not good I also see as good
Thus obtaining[13] goodness
Trustworthy people I see as good
Untrustworthy people I also see as good
Thus obtaining trust
The wise person's way in the world is to be obliging
And towards everyone he tones down his mind
so people will all listen and look to him
The wise person treats everyone as children

出生入死
生之徒十有三
死之徒十有三
人之生動之死地十有三
夫何故以其生生之厚
蓋聞善攝生者
陸行不遇兕虎
入軍不被甲兵
兕無所投其角
虎無所措其爪
兵無所容其刃
夫何故
以其無死地

德

50

Coming out in life is going into death
Three out of ten are disciples of life
Three out of ten are disciples of death
In their life three out of ten people
activate their place for death
How can this be? Because their life is lived boldly!
You may have heard that
those who are good at preserving health when walking
on the land will not meet rhinos and tigers
When joining the army
they do not wear armour and weapons
Rhinos have no place to attack with their horn
Tigers have no place to scratch with their claws
Weapons have no place to cut with their edge
Why is this so?
Because they have no place for death in them

道生之
德畜之
物形之
勢成之
是以萬物莫不尊道而貴德
道之尊
德之貴
夫莫之命常自然
故道生之
德畜之
長之育之
亭之毒之
養之覆之
生而不有
為而不恃
長而不宰
是謂玄德

德

51

They are born by The Way
nurtured by the power
matter gives them shape
and strength completes them
This is why among all things no one does not
respect The Way and honour Virtuous Power
The respect for The Way
and the honour for Virtuous Power
none of these are demanded but always given freely
Thus The Way gives them life
Virtuous Power nurtures them
raises them
fosters them
rears them
matures them
brings them up
takes them under the wing
To give life but not wanting to possess
To act without expectations
To raise but not slaughter
This is what we call the elusive Virtuous Power

天下有始
以為天下母
既知其母
復知其子
既知其子
復守其母
沒其不殆
塞其兌閉其門
終身不勤
開其兌濟其事
終身不救
見小曰明
守柔曰強
用其光復歸其明
無遺身殃
是為習常

52

The world has a beginning
We consider it to be the mother of all things
By knowing the mother
we can return to know the child
By knowing the child
we can return to cherish the mother
Without her there is no beginning[14]
Block your senses and close the gate
and you will not deplete yourself all life
Open your senses and succeed with affairs
and you can never be rescued
To see the small is called being enlightened
To keep the softness is called strength
Use the brightness and return to the light
Do not abandon yourself and bring in calamity
This is to be proficient at constancy

使我介然有知
行於大道
唯施是畏
大道甚夷
而民好徑
朝甚除
田甚蕪
倉甚虛
服文綵
帶利劍
厭飲食
財貨有餘
是謂盜夸
非道也哉

德

53

If we have a bit of knowledge
we walk The Great Way
The only fear would be to sway
The Great Way is very even
but people like shortcuts
The court is neat and tidy
The fields are very overgrown
Warehouses are completely empty
Clothes are of sophisticated silk
A sharp sword in the belt
Satiated with food and drink
Wealth and goods are plentiful
This is bragging to be a thief
and this is not The Way!

113

善建不拔
善抱者不脫
子孫以祭祀不輟
修之於身其德乃真
修之於家其德乃餘
修之於鄉其德乃長
修之於國其德乃豐
修之於天下其德乃普
故
以身觀身
以家觀家
以鄉觀鄉
以國觀國
以天下觀天下
吾何以知天下然哉
以此

德

Well erected cannot be uprooted
Those who are good at keeping will not let it slip
The ancestor sacrifices will not cease to be performed
Cultivate it in yourself and Virtuous Power will be inherent
Cultivate it in the family and Virtuous Power will be ample
Cultivate it in the village and Virtuous Power will be far reaching
Cultivate it in the country and Virtuous Power will be abundant
Cultivate it in the world and Virtuous Power will be widespread
Therefore
Perceive yourself by looking at yourself
Perceive the family by looking at the family
Perceive the village by looking at the village
Perceive the country by looking at the country
Perceive the world by looking at the world
How can I know that the world is so?
From this

含德之厚
比於赤子
蜂蠆虺蛇不螫
猛獸不據
攫鳥不搏
骨弱筋柔而握固
未知牝牡之合而全作
精之至也
終日號而不嗄
和之至也
知和曰常
知常曰明
益生曰祥
心使氣曰強
物壯則老
謂之不道
不道早已

He who has ample Virtuous Power
is like a new born baby
Wasps scorpions or poisonous snakes will not bite him
Wild beasts do not pounce upon him
Birds of prey will not strike down on him
His bones are weak and the tendons are soft
but he has a firm grip
He is not yet aware of the union of man and woman
yet he can fully erect
This means his inner life force is at its highest
He can scream all day long yet does not become hoarse
This means he is extremely harmonious
To know harmony is constancy
To know constancy is to be enlightened
The increasing after being born is actually a bad omen
Controlling the breath with the mind is forcing it
When things have grown to be strong they get old
We say this is not The Way
What is not The Way is soon going to end

知者不言
言者不知
塞其兌
閉其門
挫其銳
解其紛
和其光
同其塵
是謂玄同
故
不可得而親
不可得而疏
不可得而利
不可得而害
不可得而貴
不可得而賤
故為天下貴

Those who know do not speak
Those who speak do not know
Block your senses
Close the gate
It softens the edges
Untangles the entangled[15]
Softens the sunlight
Settles the dust
This is called the mysterious unity
You cannot take it and make it come close or leave it
You cannot take it and make it useful or harmful
You cannot take it and make it valuable or worthless
This is why it is the most precious thing in the world

以正治國
以奇用兵
以無事取天下
吾何以知其然哉
以此
天下多忌諱而民彌貧
民多利器國家滋昏
人多伎巧奇物滋起
法令滋彰盜賊多有
故聖人云
我無為而民自化
我好靜而民自正
我無事而民自富
我無欲而民自樸

德

57

With correctness you rule the country
Be unpredictable when deploying troops
Take the world by doing nothing
How can I know this is correct?
From this
The more taboos and prohibitions
the more poor people there will be
The more fine weapons the people have
the more the nation's families will find themselves in dark times
The more clever and intelligent people are
the more odd things will be made
The more laws and edicts
the more robbers and thieves there will be
Therefore the wise person says
I do not act and people will change themselves
I like peace and people behave correctly by themselves
I do not have any affairs and people prosper by themselves
I have no desires
and the people will see the value of simplicity themselves

其政悶悶
其民淳淳
其政察察
其民缺缺
禍兮福之所倚
福兮禍之所伏
孰知其極
其無正
正復為奇
善復為妖
人之迷其日固久
是以聖人
方而不割
廉而不劌
直而不肆
光而不耀

德

58

If the government is bewildered
the people are honest and sincere
If the government is watchful
the people are fallible
Yes misfortune is what good fortune relies on
Yes good fortune is what harbours misfortune
Who knows what is the finest?
That is being not correct
Correctness turns around and becomes something warped
Excellence turns around and becomes cunning
The People's delusion has lasted for a good long time
Therefore the wise person
surrounds the enemy but does not cut them down
corners the enemy but does not stab them
straightens things out but not perfectly
is enlightening but not blinding

治人事天莫若嗇
夫唯嗇是謂早服
早服謂之重積德
重積德則無不克
無不克則莫知其極
莫知其極可以有國
有國之母可以長久
是謂深根固柢
長生久視之道

德

59

When ruling the people and serving Heaven
nothing is more important than being provident
Only this can be said to be restoring ahead of time
Restoring ahead of time
is to give importance to accruing power
When you give importance to accruing power
there is nothing you cannot achieve
When there is nothing you cannot achieve
no one knows your limitation
When no one knows your limitation
you can possess a country
When you know the basic principles
of possessing a country your reign can last long
This is called having a deep root and a solid foundation
The Way of having long life with good eyesight

治大國若烹小鮮
以道蒞天下
其鬼不神
非其鬼不神
其神不傷人
非其神不傷人
聖人亦不傷人
夫兩不相傷
故德交歸焉

德

60

Ruling a great country is like cooking a small fish[16]
If the world is guided by The Way
evil ghosts will not be regarded as deities
If evil ghosts are not regarded as deities
then no deities will be regarded as harmful to people
If no deities are regarded as harmful to people
then the wise person will also not be regarded
as harmful to people
If the two do not damage each other
then Virtuous Power may be reinstated from their cooperation

大國者下流
天下之交
天下之牝
牝常以靜勝
牡以靜為下
故大國以下小國
則取小國
小國以下大國
則取大國
故
或下以取
或下而取
大國不過欲兼畜人
小國不過欲入事人
夫兩者各得其所欲
大者宜為下

A great country is like a river that flows low
everything flows into and merges with it
Just like the females of the world
The female always uses peace to win over the male
Because the female is peaceful she is considered inferior
Thus it is that
a big country by placing itself below a small country
can assimilate the small country
The small country by being small will become a big country
and has in fact assimilated the big country
Thus some place themselves below to conquer
Some conquer by being below
A great country only concerns itself
with its desire to raise the whole population
A small country only concerns itself
with going into the service of others
That way both parties get what they want
So for the great it is very appropriate to be below

道者萬物之奧
善人之寶
不善人之所保
美言可以市
尊行可以加人
人之不善何棄之有
故立天子置三公
雖有拱璧以先駟馬
不如坐進此道
古之所以貴此道者何
不曰以求得
有罪以免耶
故為天下貴

德

62

The Way is a profound place in all things
It is what admirable people value highly
and it is what protects less admirable people
Beautiful words can be used for negotiating on a marketplace
and respectful behaviour can improve people
So why should we discard that which not so admirable
people have to offer?
Thus when instating the Son of Heaven and the three ministers
even if they get precious symbols of rank and luxurious carriages
this is not as fine as teaching them to sit and approach The Way
So what is it about The Way that the ancients valued so greatly?
Did they not say "search and you shall find"?
and "the guilty should be forgiven"?
This is why everyone values it dearly

為無為
事無事
味無味
大小多少
報怨以德
圖難於其易
為大於其細
天下難事必作於易
天下大事必作於細
是以聖人終不為大
故能成其大
夫輕諾必寡信
多易必多難
是以聖人猶難之
故終無難矣

德

63

Act effortlessly
Serve without serving
Taste without tasting
Make the small great and the few numerous
Return hate with Virtuous Power
Plan the difficult like it was easy
Do great things as if they were nothing
All difficult things in the world must be done with ease
All great things must be done like they were nothing
Therefore the wise person never does anything great
That is why he is able to complete great things
He who easily makes promises has little credibility
He who regards things as very easy
will encounter great difficulty
This is why the wise person always regards things as difficult
and therefore never has difficulties

其安易持
其未兆易謀
其脆易泮
其微易散
為之於未有
治之於未亂
合抱之木生於毫末
九層之臺起於累土
千里之行始於足下
為者敗之
執者失之
是以聖人
無為故無敗
無執故無失
民之從事常於幾成而敗之
慎終如始則無敗事
是以聖人欲不欲
不貴難得之貨
學不學
復眾人之所過
以輔萬物之自然
而不敢為

What is peaceful is easy to control
What there is no sign of yet is easy to plan for
What is brittle is easy to break
Act when it has not yet manifested
Control it when there is not yet chaos
A tree that you can reach around
is born from a hair thin sprout
A nine stories tower
is raised from a pile of soil
A journey of one thousand miles starts by taking a step
He who interferes with something ruins it
He who grasps something loses it
This is why the wise person
does not act and therefore has no failures
does not grasp and therefore loses nothing
The enterprises that people are undertaking
how many are nearly accomplished when they ruin it?
If you are as attentive in the end as in the beginning
there would be no affairs that would go wrong
This is why the wise person wants to be without desires
He does not value rare goods
He has learned not to study
and thus returns to that which other people overlook
and with this he assists the natural course of all things
so he does not dare to interfere

古之善為道者
非以明民
將以愚之
民之難治
以其智多
故以智治國
國之賊
不以智治國
國之福
知此兩者亦稽式
常知稽式
是謂玄德
玄德深矣遠矣
與物反矣
然後乃至大順

德

65

That the ancients were good at living the Way
was because they did not seek to enlighten the people
but wanted to keep them ignorant
What makes people difficult to rule is
that they have knowledge
Therefore ruling a country with knowledge
is a country's detriment
Ruling a country without knowledge
is a country's good fortune
Always be aware that these two rules
are in fact basic principles
Always being aware of these basic principles
is called the elusive Virtuous Power
The elusive Virtuous Power is deep and far reaching
It turns everything upside down
and then we can come to the great realization

江海所以能為百谷王者
以其善下之
故能為百谷王
是以聖人欲上民
必以言下之
欲先民
必以身後之
是以聖人
處上而民不重
處前而民不害
是以天下樂推而不厭
以其不爭
故天下莫能與之爭

德

66

The reason that the river and the sea
can be the king of a hundred valleys
is their ability to be under them
That is how they can be the king of a hundred valleys
Therefore when the wise person wants to stand above people
he must use words that are under them
If he wants to be before people
he must place himself behind them
This enables the wise person to
place himself above and people will not feel oppressed
place himself before and people will not be harmed
This will make the whole world happily push him
forward without resentment
Because he does not dispute
in all the world no one is able to argue with him

天下皆謂我道大似不肖
夫唯大故似不肖
若肖久矣
其細也夫
我有三寶
持而保之
一曰慈
二曰儉
三曰不敢為天下先
慈故能勇
儉故能廣
不敢為天下先
故能成器長
今舍慈且勇
舍儉且廣
舍後且先
死矣夫
慈以戰則勝
以守則固
天將救之以慈衛之

德

67

Everybody says my Way is great
although it does not appear to be so
It is only because it is great that it does not appear to be so
If it had looked great it would have ended long ago
This is indeed being very small
I have three treasures which I keep and defend
The first is compassion
The second is frugality
The third is not daring to be in the front in the world
If I am compassionate I can be brave
If I am frugal I can be generous
If I do not dare to be in front in the world
I can become manager of the armoury
Now if I gave up being compassionate and was brave
Gave up being frugal and was generous
Gave up being behind and was in the front
I would already be dead
Using compassion in battle I would win
When Heaven wants to spare somebody
it uses compassion to protect them

善為士者不武
善戰者不怒
善勝敵者不與
善用人者為之下
是謂不爭之德
是謂用人之力
是謂配天古之極

德

68

Excellent officers do not battle
Excellent fighters are not aggressive
Excellent slayers do not partake
Excellent employers are humble
This is the Virtuous Power of no resistance
This is utilizing people's powers
This is following the ultimate ancient purpose of Heaven

用兵有言
吾不敢為主而為客
不敢進寸而退尺
是謂
行無行
攘無臂
扔無敵
執無兵
禍莫大於輕敵
輕敵幾喪吾寶
故抗兵相加
哀者勝矣

There is a saying about deploying troops
I do not dare to be the host only the guest
I do not dare to advance an inch only retreat a foot
This we call
Marching without marching
Pulling up the sleeves without using the arm
Throwing against no enemy
Taking control without weapons
There is no greater mistake than
underestimating your enemy
Underestimating the enemy
how many of my treasures will I lose?
Thus when in combat soldiers increase the fight against each other
the mourners will be the only winners

吾言甚易知甚易行
天下莫能知莫能行
言有宗事有君
夫唯無知是以不我知
知我者希則我者貴
是以聖人被褐懷玉

德

My words are very easy to understand
and very easy to apply
But nobody in the world can understand them
and no one can apply them
Words have a purpose
Affairs have a lord
It is just because they do not understand
that they do not understand me
Those who understand me are rare
so those who follow me are valuable
Therefore the wise person dresses shabbily
to hide his splendour

知不知上
不知知病
夫唯病病
是以不病
聖人不病
以其病病
是以不病

德

71

Knowing that you do not know is above all
Not knowing that you know is also a mistake
Precisely because mistakes are recognized as mistakes
will make you faultless
That the wise person is without faults
is because he sees mistakes as mistakes
That makes him faultless

149

民不畏威
則大威至
無狎其所居
無厭其所生
夫唯不厭
是以不厭
是以聖人
自知不自見
自愛不自貴
故去彼取此

德

72

When the people do not fear power
then greater power is applied
But there should be no imposing on their dwellings
no hostility towards their life
Only by not being hostile
can you make them not hostile
This is why the wise person
knows himself but do not show himself
Loves himself but is not vainglorious
Thus discarding one thing and keeping the other

勇於敢則殺
勇於不敢則活
此兩者或利或害
天之所惡孰知其故
是以聖人猶難之
天之道
不爭而善勝
不言而善應
不召而自來
繟然而善謀
天網恢恢
踈而不失

德

73

Those who have the courage to dare will be killed
Those who have the courage to not dare will live
Of these two one is beneficial the other harmful
When Heaven disapproves of something
who can tell the reason?
Thus the wise person still regards this to be a difficult matter
The Way of Heaven
does not fight but is excellent at winning
does not speak but is excellent at responding
does not call but people come by themselves
Is relaxed[17] but make excellent plans
The net of Heaven is vast
although its mesh is big it lets nothing escape

民不畏死
奈何以死懼之
若使民常畏死而為奇者
吾得執而殺之孰敢
常有司殺者殺
夫司殺者是大匠斲
夫代大匠斲者
希有不傷其手矣

德

74

People do not fear death
so it would be to no avail using death as deterrent
If we could make people constantly fear death
and make them take it seriously
we could arrest and kill them
Then who would dare?
There is the office of executions
that takes care of the that
They are great artisans
Those who cut wood instead of a good artisan
will only end up cutting their own arm

民之飢以其上食稅之多
是以飢
民之難治以其上之有為
是以難治
民之輕死以其求生之厚
是以輕死
夫唯無以生為者
是賢於貴生

德

75

That people are starving
is because of the heavy food taxes collected by the superiors
That is the cause of hunger
That people are difficult to control
is because of the actions of the superiors
That is why people are difficult to control
That people take death lightly
is because of the burden of trying to survive
Only those who do not regard life
as something that should be manipulated
are being virtuous and cherishing life

人之生也柔弱
其死也堅強
萬物草木之生也柔脆
其死也枯槁
故堅強者死之徒
柔弱者生之徒
是以
兵強則不勝
木強則共
強大處下
柔弱處上

德

76

When people are born they are soft and weak
When they die they become hard and stiff
When all kinds of plants and trees are alive
they are soft and crisp
When they die they are dry and wilt
Thus it is that
those that are hard and stiff are disciples of death
those that are soft and weak are disciples of life
Thus soldiers that are strong and unyielding
will not be victorious
and trees that are strong and unyielding
will be put to good use
Strong and great is inferior
Soft and weak is superior

天之道其猶張弓與
高者抑之
下者舉之
有餘者損之
不足者補之
天之道損有餘而補不足
人之道則不然
損不足以奉有餘
孰能有餘以奉天下
唯有道者
是以聖人
為而不恃
功成而不處
其不欲見賢

德

77

The Way of Heaven is like pulling a bow
If the aim is too high you lower it
If the aim is too low you raise it
If there is too much tension you decrease it
If there is not enough tension you increase it
The Way of Heaven is to
decrease the excess and
increase the insufficient
The Way of man is not like that
It decreases the insufficient by giving in to the excessive
Who is able to have excess by giving away to everyone?
Only those who have The Way
Therefore the wise person
acts but does not rely on a result
Complete the task but does not dwell on it
He does not desire recognition of his talents

天下莫柔弱於水
而攻堅強者莫之能勝
其無以易之
弱之勝強
柔之勝剛
天下莫不知
莫能行
是以聖人云
受國之垢
是謂社稷主
受國不祥
是謂天下王
正言若反

德

78

In the whole world nothing is as soft and weak as water
but when it comes to attacking the hard and strong
nothing surpasses it
The reason is that you cannot take its place
Weak overcomes strong
Soft overcomes hard
Everyone knows this
but no one is able to apply it
This is why the wise person says
He who will assume the disgrace of the country
is the master of the land and harvest sacrifice
He who will assume the misfortune of the country
is king of the world
These correct statements may seem contradictory

和大怨必有餘怨
安可以為善
是以聖人執左契
而不責於人
有德司契
無德司徹
天道無親
常與善人

德

79

After reconciling great disagreements
there is always some resentment left
Peace can be seen as good
This is why the virtuous person
keeps the left side of the contract
but does not make claims against people
Those who are virtuous maintain the contract
While those who are not virtuous will keep demanding
The Way of Heaven has no favourites
but is always with the good person

小國寡民
使有什伯之器而不用
使民重死
而不遠徙
雖有舟輿
無所乘之
雖有甲兵
無所陳之
使民復結繩而用之
甘其食
美其服
安其居
樂其俗
鄰國相望
雞犬之聲相聞
民至老死
不相往來

德

80

Keep the country small and the people few in number
Let there be smaller armed groups
but do not use them
Make people fear death
but do not scare them away
Although having boats and carriages
there should be nowhere they want to go with them
Although there are armoured soldiers
there should be nowhere to deploy them
Make people go back to
Counting their money and spending it
Making their food tasty
Making their clothes beautiful
Making peaceful homes
Making music for traditional occasions
Neighbouring lands are within sight and
the sounds of each other's chickens and dogs can be heard
The countries' people reach old age
Minding their own business

信言不美
美言不信
善者不辯
辯者不善
知者不博
博者不知
聖人不積
既以為人
己愈有
既以與人
己愈多
天之道
利而不害
聖人之道
為而不爭

81

Trustworthy words are not beautiful
Beautiful words are not trustworthy
Good people do not argue
People who argue are not good
Those who have knowledge are not wealthy
Those who are wealthy have no knowledge
Wise people do not hoard
The more they do for other people
the more they have themselves
The more they give other people
the more they get themselves
The Way of Heaven
is to profit without causing harm
The Way of the wise person
is to act without causing resistance[18]

Notes

1. The concept of The Way has huge philosophical and religious connotations today ranging from the most traditional Daoist sects to the New Age community, and it has been discussed by laymen, scholars and priests for many centuries, and this situation may have muddled the waters. Probably the most common translation of the first line 道可道非常道 is *The Way that can be spoken of is not the Eternal Way.*
However, neither speak of, nor eternal are very common meanings of these characters, and the grammar is unusual.
At the time the Dao De Jing was written the concept of The Way was still rather new. I find it very logical that the meaning of the first sentence is a simple explanation saying that the idea of The Way is not a common road. This implies, of course, that The Way is something else.

In the Zhou period the most common meanings of 道 were *way, road, method, principle, show the way, lead, explain, speak.*
In the Zhou period the most common meanings of 常 were *constant, daily, often, regularly, common, ordinary, perpetuate, always.*

There cannot be much doubt that the first 名 is a noun meaning *a name* in this context. However, the second 名 is a verb and in this function it can mean to *name*, to *call*, to *say*, to *give a name*, to *know as*, to *designate*, to *command*.

The structure of the two first lines is exactly the same where 可 and 非 常 is repeated, and therefore they must be translated the same way. If common is chosen for the first line this leaves only one possible translation for the second line:
名可名非常名 *A name can name it but it is not an common name.* The idea seems to be that "The Way" may be used as a name, but it does not cover the whole idea in itself. And this is, of course, what the 37 verses about Dao are elaborating on in the first part of the book.
Only one of the excavated copies, from the Mawangdui site, had this line intact. It is slightly different using "heng" 道可道也，非恆道也 but the meaning is exactly the same.

2. The only other pre-Han text where straw dogs are mentioned is in the Zhuang Zi. It seems they were meticulously prepared for the ceremony but discarded after, thus describing a heartless attitude toward things that are no longer of any use.

3. 爭 can mean *to fight* both physically and verbally. In this case either would be too limiting.

4. The sentence 絕學無憂 traditionally belongs as the first in chapter 20. However, it is very obvious from the context that it is, in fact, the last line of chapter 19.

5. Regarding the two words 唯 and 阿, they are in this sentence onomatopoeic words meaning something like 'yeah' and 'aye'. Many translations have yes and no but there are no cases in ancient texts to support this idea.

6. This sentence is translated very differently in various translations; like *warm-cold, work-rest* etc. There is no help to find in the excavated versions and there really are only a few possibilities which are close to common use in ancient texts that could fit the present context of little and big:

   a. 歔 means to *snort* - 吹 means *to blow with the mouth*. This does not fit the pattern of the context where big is first - since snorting should be lesser than blowing. Anyway it is difficult to see the meaning.

   b. 歔 could perhaps mean *to breathe through the nose* and 吹 could perhaps mean *to breathe through the mouth*. However, 歔 does not commonly mean *breathe*, only *snivel* or *snort*. But 歔吹 could make sense if viewed as being able to breathe through the nose as opposed to breathing through the mouth - meaning breathing normally as opposed to being out of breathe.

   c. 歔 means *to snivel*. If 吹 is a mistake and the correct character is 欷, 歔欷 would mean *little-* and *big crying*. 歔欷 is very common together meaning to *snivel and sob*. I haven't been able to find any instances in databases of ancient texts of 歔 and 吹 together or even in the same sentence displaying opposites. Therefore I believe the right character could, in fact, be 欨.

Although option 1 is straight from the dictionary it makes no sense. The best choice seems to be either option 2 or 3. Although option 2 could be a possibility, breathing through the nose while others are panting seems to be a long stretch. Therefore I have chosen option 3 because I find it more plausible that 吹 not only means *blow* but also *sob*. And there is a suitable contrast between *snivel* and *sob loudly*.

However, we must accept that there is no certain translation possible for this sentence at the present.

7. The Mawangdui text has 不忘 *not be forgotten* instead of 不亡 *not perish*. The difference is easy to see; 不亡 would be that the soul lives on, 不忘 that one's reputation lives on. Therefore I stay with 不亡 of the received version.

Taking the spiritual nature of the text into consideration I find it most reasonable to translate 壽 as eternal life because long life would make little sense if the person is dead.

8. There can be no doubt whatsoever that in the Dao De Jing 德 means *power* - The power of governing. However, there is a distinction that cannot be expressed in one word in English. It must be discerned. This chapter, the first in the book of De, explains very clearly what it is.

In the present chapter it is obvious that the author talks about two kinds of Power. 德 is not only the broad concept of power and it is not only virtue. It is both. Sometimes power is wrong sometimes very good and reasonable. Thus, in English I feel I have no choice but to add Virtuous to Power to discern the good power from the bad power. And, in fact, Virtuous is a very common definition of 德 in many classical texts.

9. In this chapter I am convinced by the obvious context that 德 is referring to virtue as morality more than power.

10. In the last sentence 善始且成 I have replaced 貸 with 始 because

in this case the line in the Mawangdui copy is the only thing that makes sense.

11. 強梁 is often translated as a compound meaning *being violent*. However, there are actually very few examples of this in early texts to compare with, and most have some connection to this sentence. The two words mean *strength* and *upholding*. I don't believe that it means being violent, but to use unyielding strength in ones life - as opposed to the non-action of The Way.

12. I assume that riding-horses, as opposed to work-horses, are not strong enough for pulling the ploughs but can be used for lighter farm work.

13. In both 德善 and 德信 I read 德 as 得.

14. 沒其不殆: 其 is often replaced with 身 in this sentence because there is really no way to make sense of it. However, I believe that it is actually 殆 which is the mistake: 始 and 殆 is obviously very close in appearance - in seal script they look like this: 𦕅 𦕅. In contrast 其身 are not as close 𦐇 𦐇.
So, the meaning is not danger 殆 but beginning 始 which fits much better with the theme of the chapter, especially the first line where 始 also appears.

15. This sentence should obviously be identical with the one in chapter four. Therefore I have replaced 分 with 紛.

16. The analogy of cooking small fish is not directly explained in this chapter. The problems of cooking fish are usually that it can easily cook too long and be ruined, stirring the pot will cause the fish to fall apart. It is logical to assume that 'Ruling a great country is like cooking small fish' means not to overdo it - like it is often the case in the Dao De Jing - and this line is indeed very famous. However, it seems difficult to relate it to the rest of the chapter where the meaning seems to be that if The Way is the guiding principle people will not worship false deities but follow nature and genuine good spirits. The wise person, who knows

The Way and follows nature and simplicity, is perhaps not always taken seriously by people who want "real" gods to worship. The meaning of this is quite easy to determine. But it seems completely unrelated to the wonderful 'cooking small fish' analogy.

I suspect that this line could, in fact, be a one-line poem on its own, or belonging elsewhere. Therefore, I have placed it a few lines apart from the rest.

17. The received version has 繹 which means *a slack string* or *relax*. The Mawangdui version has 彈 which means *missile, ball shaped thing, shoot, catapult* among other meanings which do not seem to fit in here.

18. 爭 can mean *to fight* both physically and verbally. In this case either would be too limiting. I find it only natural that 為而不爭 is referring to *avoiding action when there is resistance*.

www.ingramcontent.com/pod-product-compliance
Lightning Source LLC
Chambersburg PA
CBHW070024050525
26173CB00006B/148